MICHAEL JACKSON

ULTIMATE MUSIC LEGEND

MICHAEL JACKSON

ULTIMATE MUSIC LEGEND

Katherine Krohn

LERNER PUBLICATIONS COMPANY · MINNEAPOLIS

This book is dedicated to my dad, Don Krohn, M.D., who ushered the babies of several Motown luminaries into the world.

Lerner Publications Company
A division of Lerner Publishing Group, Inc.
241 First Avenue North
Minneapolis, MN 55401 U.S.A.

Website address: www.lernerbooks.com

Library of Congress Cataloging-in-Publication Data

Krohn, Katherine E.
    Michael Jackson : ultimate music legend / by Katherine Krohn.
        p.   cm. — (Gateway biographies)
    Includes bibliographical references and index.
    ISBN 978–0–7613–5762–9 (lib. bdg. : alk. paper)
    1. Jackson, Michael, 1958–2009—Juvenile literature. 2. Rock musicians—United States—Biography—Juvenile literature. I. Title.
    ML3930.J25K76 2010
    782.42166092—dc22 [B]   2009038872

Manufactured in the United States of America
1 – BP – 12/15/09

CONTENTS

Ten-year-old Michael Jackson *(front)* poses with his older brothers *(clockwise from left)* Tito, Jackie, Jermaine, and Marlon.

Eight-year-old Michael Jackson stood in front of the audience gathered at Roosevelt High School in Gary, Indiana, in 1966. "The Jacksons"—Michael and his brothers Jackie, Tito, Jermaine, and Marlon—were competing in a citywide talent show at the school. Young Michael looked adorable with his easy smile and big, bright eyes. Sharing vocals with his brother Jermaine, Michael crooned "My Girl," a song made famous by the Temptations.

When the Jacksons finished their song, the audience gave them a standing ovation. The judges at the show gave them first prize. After the show, the excited boys took turns holding the big trophy they had won.

All the Jackson boys were talented, but Michael stood out onstage. His high, clear voice had the emotional depth of a much older person. His body moved with the grace and rhythm of an experienced dancer. He was joyful and confident. The gifted young boy loved performing, and it showed.

Life on Jackson Street

On August 29, 1958, a cute baby boy with big brown eyes was born to Joseph and Katherine Jackson of Gary, Indiana. They named him Michael Joseph Jackson. Michael had six older siblings: Maureen, Jackie, Tito, Jermaine, LaToya, and Marlon. Three years after Michael was born, Randy joined the family. Janet was born five years after that.

The Jacksons lived in a small white house on 2300 Jackson Street. It was just a coincidence that the Jacksons lived on a street that shared their family name. Joseph (Joe) Jackson worked as a crane operator at a steel mill in Gary. Katherine worked at Sears.

Both of Michael's parents were musical. Joe and

Michael and his siblings grew up in this house in Gary, Indiana.

Michael's parents, Joe and Katherine Jackson

his brother were guitar players in a local R & B (rhythm and blues) band called the Falcons. Katherine played both the piano and clarinet, and she had a beautiful singing voice. Katherine sang to Michael when he was a child. Tunes such as "You Are My Sunshine" and "Cotton Fields" were favorites. Michael adored his mother.

Michael didn't feel as close to his father, but he admired his musical talent. Every weekend, the Falcons would rehearse in the Jacksons' living room. Michael's older brothers Jackie, Tito, and Jermaine liked to watch the Falcons practice.

Joe's guitar was precious to him, and he told his kids not to touch it. But sometimes, when Joe was at work, they sneaked the guitar from its place in a closet. They'd try to play along with songs on the radio or record player. Tito was especially interested in the guitar. At first, his guitar playing wasn't very good, but he got better over time.

One day when Tito was playing the guitar, something unexpected happened. A string broke! He didn't know what to do, so he put the guitar back in the closet. He and his brothers waited nervously for their dad to come home from work and discover the broken string. That evening Joe sternly approached the boys' room with his guitar. He found Tito in the room, crying. Joe demanded to know who had been playing his guitar. Tito nervously confessed. He explained that he and his brothers had been borrowing the guitar to practice on it.

Instead of getting angry, Joe asked Tito to play him something on the guitar. Tito began to play a song he had been working on. His siblings and mother gathered in the doorway of the room to listen too. Tito was good! Joe could see that the boys had taken the guitar seriously. It wasn't a toy to them.

One evening Joe was late getting home from work. When he arrived, he was carrying a shiny red electric guitar. At first, the boys thought their dad had bought the new guitar for himself. But the guitar wasn't his, he announced. The guitar was for Tito. He told Tito that he had to share it with any of his siblings who were willing to practice. The boys were thrilled. The guitar was much more than a simple gift. Their father had opened up a world of music for them.

"Climb Ev'ry Mountain"

Michael's brothers began to rehearse regularly. Maureen and the other kids were musical too. But it was the older Jackson boys who came together to form a band. Marlon, five, joined the band playing the bongo drums. Four-year-old Michael wanted to be in the band too, but they told him he was too young.

From an early age, Michael liked to sing, and he had natural talent. When Michael was in first grade, he performed in a talent show at his school, Garrett Elementary. He wanted to look good for the event. He wore new black pants and a white shirt. Standing in the grade school auditorium, in front of students, teachers, and families, he sang "Climb Ev'ry Mountain" from *The Sound of Music*. His strong singing voice, a young boy's high soprano, had a sweet tone. When he finished his song, the whole auditorium clapped and cheered. Some of the teachers were so moved, they were crying. Michael didn't understand why everyone was acting so strangely. For him, singing was as natural as breathing. But he was glad to make people happy with his singing.

After hearing Michael perform at the school, his brothers asked him to join their band. Michael was elated. Finally! He could be in the band! He was ready. He could already sing. Like Marlon, he started out in the band playing the bongo drums.

Joe took whatever money he could save to buy more instruments and equipment for his kids. He bought a tambourine, a bass guitar, a microphone, and an amplifier. He wanted the boys to compete in talent shows and perform in public. He had a feeling they could make it big.

Because Joe wanted Michael and his brothers to succeed, he pushed them hard. He made them rehearse every day after school. Sometimes they'd have to rehearse before school too.

Later in his life, Michael Jackson claimed that his father had been abusive to him. Sometimes during rehearsals, Joe would stand nearby with a belt in his hand. If anybody goofed up, Joe hit them with the belt. Michael and his brothers lived in fear of not being perfect onstage. Joe was also critical of the way his sons looked. He often made fun of Michael's nose, which Joe said was too big. As a result, Michael felt self-conscious about it.

In spite of the harsh treatment, Michael later did acknowledge some positive things about his dad. Michael credited his father with teaching him important life lessons. For example, Joe taught Michael and his siblings how to plan and prepare for the things you want in life. Joe also taught his kids lessons about being a performer, such as how to correctly use a microphone and how to connect with an audience.

Being in a band was fun for Michael, but it was also hard work. Sometimes Michael looked at his school friends with envy. Other kids could play after school instead of spending long hours in rehearsal.

When Michael did have free time, he was like any other kid. He loved candy—especially bubble gum. He liked to play pranks on his brothers and sisters. His favorite board game was Monopoly. He liked to watch cartoons on TV. *The Road Runner Show* was his favorite.

Amateur Night

After many rehearsals, Joe decided the boys were ready to perform publicly. Calling the band the Jacksons, he signed them up for every talent show in the area. At first the boys were nervous about performing for an audience. But after winning a citywide competition at Tito's high school in 1966, they felt more confident.

People seemed to like their songs and their style. While they sang and played their instruments, they performed dance routines. Joe entered his sons in talent competitions all around Indiana. When the boys had a show coming up, their teachers would give them homework to do on the road. No matter how many shows they had to perform, the boys were expected to get straight A's in school.

Onstage, eight-year-old Michael was clearly the star attraction. Because he was so young, people didn't know what to expect at first. But when he began to sing, he bowled them over with his clear, strong voice and great personality.

The boys got their first paying gig at Mr. Lucky's Lounge, a club in Gary. The job led to other gigs in local clubs. Some of the clubs were not appropriate places for children. They served alcohol and put on shows meant for adults. But Joe figured that the boys needed experience performing for an audience.

After a long day of school, the Jacksons would often go straight to rehearsal and then to a nightclub to perform. At 11 or 12 at night, Michael and his brothers would go to bed, exhausted.

One day Joe came home from work with some exciting news. One of his coworkers, Gordon Keith, had a recording studio called Steeltown Records. Keith wanted to sign the Jacksons to his record label. Michael and his brothers couldn't believe they were going to have their own record. In 1967 the band's first single, "Big Boy," was released. The song featured nine-year-old Michael as the lead singer. The song didn't spring to national success, but it got plenty of airplay in Gary.

The Jackson boys are pictured here in 1966. Michael is on the right. They sometimes performed with a drummer named Johnny Jackson *(center, on drums)*. Johnny was not related to them.

Michael's dad wanted the Jacksons to be more than a small-town act. He had his eye on nearby Chicago. Joe signed the boys up for an amateur night competition at Chicago's Royal George Theatre. The kids piled into the family's VW minibus. In less than an hour, they arrived in Chicago.

The boys won the amateur contest at the Royal. And they won it for the next two weeks as well. The Royal George Theatre had a special rule. Anyone who won the contest three weeks in a row got to perform in a concert as an opening act for a famous band. The boys were thrilled when they found out they'd be the opening act for Gladys Knight and the Pips.

Michael and his brothers had never played in front of such a big audience—nearly one thousand people! After the show, Gladys Knight talked to Joe. She thought the Jacksons had talent, and she wanted to help them. She said she'd put in a good word for them with Berry Gordy Jr., the owner of Motown Records. This company was much bigger than Steeltown. Mowtown produced some of the biggest hits of the 1960s. Joe was grateful for Gladys Knight's offer, but he didn't know if anything would come of it.

After their success at the Royal, the Jacksons landed gigs at the Regal Theater and other Chicago venues. The family sometimes drove to gigs at the Fox Theater in Detroit too, about a four-hour drive from Gary. They didn't make much money at the theaters, because they usually opened for bigger acts.

Motown Records

The Motown Record Corporation was founded in 1960 in Detroit, Michigan, by Berry Gordy Jr. Berry got the word *Motown* by combining the words *motor* and *town*. Motor Town and Motor City are common nicknames for Detroit, because it is the car-making capital of the United States.

Motown Records was the first big record label owned by an African American. The Motown label featured African American artists such as Diana Ross and the Supremes, Marvin Gaye, the Temptations, Gladys Knight and the Pips, and Stevie Wonder. The label was especially important because black music had been separate from mainstream white music. Motown Records broke down barriers for African American artists. It helped them find mainstream success.

Berry Gordy Jr.

When they weren't performing, Michael would crouch behind the stage curtain and watch hot performers of the day, such as James Brown and Jackie Wilson. These two men fascinated him. They didn't dance like anybody else.

James Brown danced as if he were possessed with untamed, animal-like energy. His legs moved lightly but seemed to be charged with electricity. He would spin fast and then smoothly change to another funky move.

Michael memorized James Brown and Jackie Wilson's dance moves. He watched the way they held their arms and shook their heads. Michael especially liked Jackie Wilson's shiny, black leather shoes. He noticed how when Wilson moved about onstage, his shiny shoes seemed to flash with the color of the stage lights. Michael wanted to wear shoes like that onstage too.

James Brown (right) shows his dance moves to talk show host Johnny Carson in 1969.

Soon Joe signed the boys up for one more amateur night competition. The Apollo Theater in New York City hosted the big league of amateur-night contests. Joe knew this could be an important step for his sons' careers. After loading up their instruments, Joe and the boys left Gary. About twelve hours later, they arrived in New York. Their reputation in Chicago had followed them to New York. Without even auditioning or competing, they were entered in the amateur finals at the theater. And even though they were competing with some of the best amateur acts around, the Jacksons won first prize.

After the competition, the Jacksons headed back to Gary. Michael felt tired but excited. He and his brothers had won contest after contest. Everywhere they played, audiences loved them. But there was something that still hadn't happened. They were waiting for a phone call from Motown Records.

The kids settled back into their routine at school. But the whole family was on edge, waiting for the telephone to ring. Every time the phone rang, the Jacksons would hope it was someone from Motown Records, wanting them to audition. But instead, it was usually a friend of one of the many Jackson kids, wanting to chat.

One day Joe announced that he had great news. A producer from *The David Frost Show* in New York City had called. He wanted the Jacksons to appear on the variety TV program in a couple of days. Someone at the Apollo Theater had told the producer about their act.

Michael and his brothers were excited. They had never been on TV! That day at school, they told their friends the good news. They got advance homework from their teachers to take on the road.

That afternoon Joe gathered the boys together. He told them that the trip to New York was canceled. The Jacksons weren't going to be on the TV show. In fact, said Joe, *he* had canceled their appearance on the program. The boys couldn't believe it. What was their dad thinking? Michael felt like crying.

He watched as his dad's serious expression turned into a smile. "Motown called," he said. The Jacksons' dream had come true!

The Jackson 5

Inside the Motown recording studio, a friendly assistant helped the boys set up for the audition. With ten-year-old Michael on lead vocals, the band opened with "Who's Lovin' You." When Michael finished his last song, he looked at the people in the recording studio. Their faces didn't show emotion. Michael couldn't help but ask them how they did. Michael's brothers quickly shushed him. They knew they had to act like professionals. A Motown executive thanked the Jacksons for coming. He said they would be in touch.

Within days, Michael and his brothers were asked to return to Motown Records. This time, they were meeting with Berry Gordy himself. Not only had the Jacksons passed their audition, said Gordy, but they were going to be very famous.

Gordy was especially impressed with young Michael's talent. "His confidence and skill as a singer was beyond his years," Gordy later said. "He had a knowingness about him that was incredible."

Motown didn't waste time. They bought the Jacksons' record contract from Steeltown Records and signed the Jackson brothers to the Motown label. They changed the name of the band too. The five brothers from Gary, Indiana, would now be called the Jackson 5.

In October 1969, the Jackson 5 released the group's first Motown single, "I Want You Back." The tune, sung by eleven-year-old Michael, rocketed to the top of the Billboard music charts. Gordy paired the Jackson 5 with Diana Ross to produce the group's very first album, *Diana Ross Presents the Jackson 5*, which was soon a top-selling record. Three more successful albums followed. The Jackson 5's first four

Diana Ross befriended the Jackson boys. She and Michael became lifelong friends.

singles hit number one on the Billboard Hot 100 music chart. The Jackson family moved to Los Angeles, California, with the encouragement of Berry Gordy. Los Angeles was a center of activity for show business, and Motown Records had a branch office in the city.

In 1970 the Jackson 5 appeared on *The Ed Sullivan Show*, a popular TV variety show. Michael, dressed in black bell-bottoms, a bright red shirt, and fringed vest, stood front and center. As he sang lead vocals on "ABC," Michael looked very happy. He wore shiny black shoes, just like the ones he had seen Jackie Wilson wear onstage. As Michael sang, his shoes shimmered in the stage lights.

Michael and his brothers were suddenly famous. Teenage girls mobbed them wherever they went. Michael's

The Jackson 5 performed on *The Ed Sullivan Show* several times. Michael *(second from right)* often wore his favorite shiny shoes when he performed.

older brothers liked the attention. Teen magazines that featured the Jackson 5 filled the newsstands. The boys' faces appeared on stickers, posters, and coloring books. Things were moving fast.

In September 1971, a cartoon, *The Jackson 5ive*, made its debut on ABC. Every Saturday morning, the family would sit in front of the TV to watch their favorite cartoons. They waited in anticipation for their own show to come on. Michael couldn't believe he was the star of his own cartoon.

The Jackson 5 made guest appearances on many TV shows. The group performed several times on *Soul Train*, a program that featured Motown and soul artists. In 1971 the Jackson 5 appeared on the *Sonny and Cher Comedy Hour*, another popular TV program. Wherever the Jackson 5 appeared, Michael stood out as the star of the show.

Michael enjoyed performing with his brothers. But at thirteen, he was ready for a change. The super-talented singer wanted to see if he could fly on his own.

Flying Solo

In 1972 Michael presented his first solo Motown album, *Got to Be There*, and his first solo single by the same name. In the following year, he released a second solo album, *Ben*. The album's hit single, about a boy's love for his pet rat, was the theme song for the movie *Ben*. Michael loved animals, and the movie was one of his favorites.

Michael at the age of thirteen in 1972, the year he began a solo singing career

Michael's brothers Jermaine and Jackie also released solo albums that year. The brothers continued to perform together as well. In June 1972, the Jackson 5 released the group's last hit album, *Looking through the Windows*. The Jackson 5 went on a worldwide tour for most of 1973. Meanwhile, Michael's third album, *Music and Me*, was released.

When Michael wasn't performing, he often felt insecure. He was getting a case of acne, and he worried that people would notice. While teenage Michael was good looking, he was no longer the "adorable" little Jackson boy. His voice was changing too. Michael had heard music industry people say that his voice might not sound as good after it changed.

Michael's confidence always returned when he performed. In November 1973, when the Jackson 5 performed the group's new single, "Dancing Machine," on *Soul Train*, Michael wowed TV viewers with his "robot dance." While sliding about the stage in step with the song's beat,

Michael moved like a robot, moving his arms, legs, hands, and neck in short jerky, mechanical movements. Young people everywhere soon copied Michael's dance.

In April 1974, the Jackson 5 began a series of shows in Las Vegas. For the first time, the show included Michael's siblings Randy, LaToya, and Janet. In the same year, Michael released two more albums, *Forever, Michael*; and an album of collected hits, *The Best of Michael Jackson*. In June the Jackson 5 released the group's last album for Motown, *Moving Violation*.

At Motown the Jackson 5 could only perform songs by other artists. The Jacksons wanted a say in the songs they sang. Michael, especially, wanted to write some of his own songs. In 1975 the Jackson 5 left Motown. The record company sued the band to keep the trademark Jackson 5 name, so the band changed its name back to the Jacksons, signing with Epic records.

In 1978 the Jacksons released the group's first Epic album, *Destiny*. It included the hit single "Blame It on the Boogie." Meanwhile, Michael was exploring new career directions. He appeared in his first film role, as the Scarecrow in *The Wiz*. The movie, based on the classic film *The Wizard of Oz*, featured an all-African American cast and starred Diana Ross.

During the making of *The Wiz*, Michael met music producer Quincy Jones. The two decided to make a record together. The result was *Off the Wall*, a blend of pop, disco, soul, and funk. Four singles on the album peaked in the music charts, including "Rock with You" and "Don't Stop

'Til You Get Enough," which were both written by Michael.

After the success of *Off the Wall*, Michael and Quincy Jones decided to team up again. They worked together day and night to create the 1982 release *Thriller*. The album produced seven number one hit singles, including "Thriller"—the song for which the album was named—and "Billie Jean." It was to become the best-selling album in history.

Thriller was groundbreaking in other ways too. In 1983, in a TV special honoring Motown Records, Michael introduced another unusual dance move—the moonwalk. While singing "Billie Jean," Michael glided backward while appearing to make forward walking motions.

The *Off the Wall* and *Thriller* albums were huge hits for Michael and helped shoot him to superstardom.

Michael performs the moonwalk onstage in 1984.

Michael's moonwalk, with its supersmooth, lengthy backward slide, quickly caught on with fans. Michael also made fashion waves during the Motown special. He dressed in what would become his trademark style, donning a black fedora hat and a single white glove.

Michael's music videos for "Billie Jean" and "Thriller" changed the music video genre. Instead of calling them videos, Michael called them short films. For the first time, music videos told stories and introduced dramatic special effects.

Michael wanted his music to unite people. He wanted all people, regardless of race, to live together in harmony. MTV (Music Television), then a fairly new company, had previously featured mainly white musicians. But Michael, with his best-selling music and groundbreaking videos, was too popular for MTV to ignore. MTV began playing

Michael's Trendsetting Style

Michael Jackson was not only a supertalented singer, composer, and dancer. He was also a fashion trendsetter. When Michael appeared in a concert or video, fans around the world copied his signature styles. They included:

- a single white sequined glove
- a black fedora
- sparkly white socks and shiny black shoes
- a red leather jacket with zippers
- ankle-length pants
- mirrored sunglasses
- military-style jackets

Michael's songs and videos, paving the way for other African American artists on MTV.

In January 1984, the Pepsi corporation hired Michael to promote its soft drink in a commercial. While filming a simulated concert, Michael's hair caught on fire. He got second-degree burns to his scalp and required surgery. After the accident, Jackson received a $1.5 million settlement from Pepsi. Michael donated the money to a center for burn victims at the Brotman Medical Center in Culver City, California. A wing of the hospital was named the Michael Jackson Burn Center.

Michael made a big business move in 1985, when he bought the copyrights to many Beatles songs for close to $47 million. In the same year, he received a Presidential Humanitarian Award from President Ronald Reagan at the White House, for his work as a spokesperson against drunk driving.

Toward the end of the year, Michael and singer Lionel Richie wrote a song to benefit victims of hunger in Africa and the United States. The 1985 release "We Are the World" featured many recording artists and raised more than $60 million for charity. Once again, Michael showed, through his music, his desire to help and unite people. The song won three Grammy Awards and was the first single in history to go multiplatinum.

Humanitarian

Five years after the release of *Thriller*, Michael released the album *Bad*. It contained five number one singles, including "Man in the Mirror" and "Dirty Diana." When performing "Smooth Criminal" from the album, Michael demonstrated his anti-gravity lean, a dance move that made him appear to defy the laws of gravity. The effect was achieved by a specially designed pair of shoes that was attached to the stage floor. He held an official U.S. patent for the shoes. Besides being a singer, songwriter, dancer, and inventor, Michael became an author too. He released his autobiography, *Moonwalk*, in 1988. In the book, Michael described his childhood, his rise to fame, and his creative projects.

In 1988 Michael purchased a 2,676-acre ranch in California. He turned Neverland Ranch into his dream home. He built an amusement park that included a Ferris wheel and a roller coaster. The ranch also had a swimming pool, ponds, fountains, and statues of children playing. Michael even had a railroad built, with a train station, real tracks, and trains. Michael wanted Neverland to be more than just a home. He wanted it to be a getaway spot for underprivileged and seriously ill children and their families. He wanted Neverland to be a place where they could come to forget about their problems for a while.

Because Michael loved animals, he created a zoo at Neverland. The zoo included Michael's pet llama and boa constrictor as well as elephants, giraffes, and tigers. Michael also adopted a chimpanzee that he rescued from a research lab. Michael named his new friend Bubbles. Bubbles became Michael's constant companion.

As Michael's fame rose to new heights, so did the media's fascination with him. Around the time that *Bad* was released, Michael began having plastic surgeries. Many of the surgeries changed the appearance of Michael's nose. Newspapers reported the changes in Michael's appearance.

Michael also began getting skin treatments. The treatments lightened his skin. Critics claimed that Michael was bleaching his skin because he didn't want to look African American. Michael strongly denied this.

In a TV interview, he explained that he had a skin disease called vitiligo. The disease caused white spots and patches to develop on his skin. To make his skin tone look more even, Michael was applying a special cream that he'd gotten from a dermatologist (skin doctor). The cream made his skin look lighter.

Michael tried to put the media's gossip out of his head. He focused on things that were important to him. He worked to raise money for charities. He also put his energy into making music. In November 1991, Michael released *Dangerous*, his second album to debut at the number one position on the Billboard 200 music chart. The record spawned many hit singles, including "Black or White," a mix of rap, hard rock, and electric dance music.

In 1992 Michael founded the Heal the World Foundation. The charity's purpose was to raise money for needy children around the world. The foundation also invited sick and underprivileged children to visit Neverland. Michael launched the *Dangerous* World Tour in June 1992. He gave all profits from the tour's sixty-seven concerts to the Heal the World Foundation. He raised millions of dollars for the organization.

In the same year, Michael visited Africa, where he was well received by fans. Because of his heritage, Michael felt a special connection to the African continent. The Ivory Coast village of Krindjabo officially crowned Michael "King Sani," the king of the Agni people, in 1992. In the years to follow, Michael kept up his relationship with the Agni.

In January 1993, Michael made headlines with his amazing performance at the halftime show of Super Bowl XXVII. He opened his performance by appearing to be shot across the football stadium and onto the stage. Surrounded by fireworks explosions, he held a statuelike pose for several minutes while the crowd cheered. When he finally broke from the pose, he sang "Jam" (a funky hip-hop tune from *Dangerous*), "Black and White," and "Billie Jean." Michael closed the half-time show with a moving rendition of "Heal the World," accompanied by thirty-five hundred Los Angeles-area children.

Michael was asked to perform at President Bill Clinton's inauguration ball in 1993. During the event,

Michael took the stage at halftime during Super Bowl XXVII in Pasadena, California.

Michael publicly asked the Clinton administration to give funding to HIV/AIDS research and charity organizations.

Ups and Downs

A cloud formed over Michael's life in 1993. That year he was accused of molesting a young boy whom he'd invited to visit Neverland. Michael denied hurting the boy, whom he had befriended. Michael's attorneys settled the case out of court, and no criminal charges were made.

The next year, Michael surprised his fans by announcing that he had been married for two months. On May 18, 1994, he had wed Lisa Marie Presley, daughter of singer Elvis Presley, in a private ceremony in the Dominican Republic. Some people said the only reason Michael had married was to try to take the focus off the molestation charges. But both Michael and Lisa Marie defended their marriage. "I'm not gonna marry somebody for any reason other than the fact that I've fallen in love with them," Lisa Marie said in an interview with ABC News.

Michael was a private person. Because he was so famous, he rarely went out in public. He spent a great deal of time at home, visiting with his family, talking on the phone, playing with his pets, and writing songs. He liked to climb trees. He had a special tree at Neverland that he called his Giving Tree. There, perched in the tree's big branches, Michael wrote the lyrics for many songs.

In June 1995, Michael released a double album called *HIStory: Past, Present, and Future.* On the hit single "Scream," Michael performed with his sister Janet. The song expressed Michael's feelings about how he was treated as a celebrity. *HIStory* became the best-selling multiple-disc album of all time.

In 1996 Michael and Lisa Marie divorced. Despite their love for each other, they just couldn't make the relationship work. On November 15, Michael married his friend, Debbie Rowe. Michael had met Debbie a few years earlier, when she was a nurse working for his dermatologist.

Michael was overjoyed when Debbie gave birth to their first child, Prince Michael Jackson Jr., in 1997. The next year, a second child, Paris Michael Katherine Jackson, was born. When Michael and Debbie divorced in 1999, the children stayed with Michael.

In September 2001, Michael was honored with a Thirtieth Anniversary Celebration at Madison Square Garden in New York City. The sold-out concert was presented on two separate days, September 7 and 10. Michael had a special surprise for his fans on the second night of the celebration. Michael and his brothers—Jermaine, Tito, Randy, Jackie, and Marlon—performed together for the first time since 1984, singing a medley of their greatest hits.

Just hours after the Jackson brothers' concert, about four miles away, terrorists flew airplanes into the twin towers of New York's World Trade Center. Michael wanted to help the victims of the terrorist attacks. He helped organized a benefit concert in Washington, D.C.

On October 21, a wide range of entertainers appeared in the televised event. Michael sang the finale at the event—his new song, "What More Can I Give."

In October, Michael released *Invincible,* his first studio album in six years. The album topped the charts in many countries.

Michael liked to spend time with his children, and he wanted his kids to have a happy childhood. Occasionally he would take Prince Michael Jr. and Paris to Disneyland or the zoo. But photographers and fans hounded the family wherever they went. Michael didn't want his children to be hurt by his star status. For the first years of their lives, he protected them as best he could from the press. When they made a rare appearance in public, he had them wear veils or face masks.

Michael greatly enjoyed being a father, and he wanted to have another child. He decided to have a baby using a surrogate mother. (A surrogate mother is a mother who has a baby for another mother

To help protect his children's identities, Michael often hid their faces when they went out in public.

or father who wants one.) In 2002 Michael announced the birth of Prince Michael Jackson II. He nicknamed the baby Blanket—a name that, for Michael, expressed the love and warmth that parents give to their children.

Michael loved his new son very much. But shortly after he was born, Michael caused controversy by holding the baby over a hotel balcony for fans gathered below to see. Later, Michael acknowledged his poor judgment and issued an apology.

Controversy swarmed around the star again in 2003, when the parents of a thirteen-year-old boy accused him of child molestation. Michael had befriended the boy and his family when the boy was diagnosed with cancer in 2000. When the boy had to have his spleen and a kidney removed, Michael had organized a blood drive, provided transportation to chemotherapy treatments, and offered financial support to the boy's family.

When the boy's parents pressed charges, seventy law enforcement officers raided and searched Michael's Neverland home. They found no evidence, but Michael still had to prove his innocence in court. He firmly denied doing anything wrong. He claimed that the boy's family was trying to get money from him by taking him to court. Two years later, the case went to trial. During the trial, Michael's health declined. He lost a great deal of weight.

At the trial, Michael's family and friends defended his innocence. A jury eventually found Michael innocent of all the charges. But many people who knew Michael said he was never the same after the trial.

Immediately following the trial, Michael and his children left Neverland, never to return. For a year, they lived in Bahrain (a country in the Persian Gulf) as guests of the country's royal family. Michael avoided the press during this time. He didn't make new recordings. Eventually he and his children returned to California.

Michael spoke with a reporter in 2007. "While some have made deliberate attempts to hurt me, I take it in stride," he said of the molestation charges. "I have a loving family, a strong faith and wonderful friends and fans who have, and continue, to support me." Surrounded by his children, other family members, and close friends, Michael lived a mostly secluded life for the next two years.

Final Curtain Call

In early 2009, Michael announced to the press that he would perform again. He would launch a series of concerts at London's 02 Arena in July. The concert series, called This Is It, had special significance. It would be Michael's "final curtain call." Michael was ready to retire from show business.

Michael, fifty years old, was slated to present fifty concerts. His fans were excited. He hadn't performed in many years. Tickets for the concert series sold out within hours.

Some people worried that Michael wasn't healthy enough to perform. In recent photos, he had appeared

Michael rehearses for his final concert series in June 2009.

thin and frail looking. Regardless, he worked hard to plan the concert and rehearse. He especially looked forward to his kids seeing the show. They had never seen their dad perform in concert.

On June 24, 2009, Michael attended a rehearsal at the Staples Center in Los Angeles. He seemed happy, and the rehearsal went well. The next day, one of Michael's staff members called paramedics to his Los Angeles home. Michael wasn't breathing. Michael's private physician, Dr. Conrad Murray, was present in his home and tried to revive him. Paramedics rushed Michael to UCLA Medical Center and tried at length to help him breathe. But he was pronounced dead at 2:26 P.M. His heart had stopped. Michael's family was with him when he died.

A coroner (official who investigates deaths) examined Michael's body and found prescription drugs in his system, including propofol. Propofol makes a person go to sleep and is typically used during surgeries. It is given intravenously (through a vein). Dr. Murray had given Michael propofol the night before he died. Michael may have been using the drug to help him sleep. People close to him said that he'd been suffering from severe insomnia. The coroner determined that the mixture of drugs in Michael's body caused his death.

When the press released the news of Michael's death, fans around the world mourned and gathered to honor his life and music. President Barack Obama remarked, "I think that Michael Jackson will go down in history as one of our greatest entertainers. I grew up on his music, still have all . . . his stuff on my iPod." On July 7, a memorial was held for Michael. It took place at the Staples Center in Los Angeles—the same place where Michael had rehearsed the day before his death. Twenty thousand tickets were issued to fans. Millions more watched the memorial live on TV and on the Internet.

Many of Michael's friends spoke at the memorial, including his longtime friend, actress Brooke Shields. But the most moving words came from Michael's eleven-year-old daughter, Paris. "Ever since I was born, Daddy has been the best father you could ever imagine," she said. "I just want to say that I love him so much."

On September 3, 2009, Michael Jackson was laid to rest in a mausoleum (aboveground cemetery) at Forest Lawn Memorial Park in Glendale, California. The next month, the film *Michael Jackson's This Is It* was released in theaters worldwide. The film features footage of

Fans leave flowers, signs, balloons, and notes for Michael Jackson at his parents' home in Los Angeles. Many people around the world mourned the famous singer's death.

Michael preparing and rehearsing for what would have been his final concert.

Michael Jackson's life was cut short, but his musical legacy is lasting. In 2007 Michael spoke to a writer for *Ebony* magazine. "Music has been my outlet, my gift to all of the lovers in this world," he said. "Through it . . . I know I will live forever."

IMPORTANT DATES

1958   Michael Joseph Jackson is born in Gary, Indiana, on August 29.

1964   He starts performing with his brothers.

1966   The Jacksons win a citywide talent show.

1967   The Jacksons cut their first record at Steeltown Records in Gary.

           The band wins an amateur-night competition at Harlem's famous Apollo Theater.

1968   The Jacksons audition for Motown Records in Detroit. After landing a record contract, the group changes its name to the Jackson 5.

1969   The Jackson 5's first full-length album is released.

1972   Michael begins his solo recording career with the release of *Got to Be There*.

1978   He plays the Scarecrow in *The Wiz*, starring Diana Ross.

1979	He releases *Off the Wall*, his first collaboration with producer Quincy Jones.
1982	He releases what will be the best-selling album of all time, *Thriller*. Seven of the album's nine songs become number one hits.
1984	During the filming of a Pepsi commercial, Michael's hair catches on fire.
1985	"We Are the World," by Michael Jackson and Lionel Richie, is released. Proceeds from the hit record are donated to famine victims in Ethiopia.
1987	His album *Bad* produces five hit singles.
1988	He releases his autobiography, *Moonwalk*. He buys Neverland Ranch.
1993	He is accused of molesting a boy who used to visit his home. The case is settled out of court, and criminal charges are not made.
1994	He marries the daughter of Elvis Presley, Lisa Marie Presley. The marriage lasts two years.

1996	He marries Debbie Rowe.
1997	Rowe gives birth to Michael's first child, Prince Michael Jackson Jr.
1998	Paris Michael Katherine Jackson is born.
1999	Michael and Debbie Rowe divorce.
2002	His third child, Prince Michael Jackson II, nicknamed Blanket, is born to an unidentified surrogate mother.
2003	Neverland Ranch is raided and searched by law enforcement officers after the parents of a thirteen-year-old boy press child molestation charges.
2005	After a difficult court battle, Michael is found innocent. He closes Neverland Ranch and leaves the country with his children.
2009	He announces that he will launch a fifty-concert tour, This Is It, in July. But on June 25, Michael dies of heart failure. His body is laid to rest in a mausoleum at Forest Lawn Memorial Park in Glendale, California, on September 3.

SOURCE NOTES

20 *People,* "From Smalltown to Motown," July 13, 2009, 64–68.

32 Pat Saperstein, "Michael Jackson Dies at 50: Pop Icon Suffers Suspected Heart Attack in L.A.," *Variety,* June 25, 2009, http://www.variety.com/article/VR1118005395.html?categoryid=3667&cs=1&query=michael+jackson+dies+at+50 (October 15, 2009).

36 Eric Talmadge, "Guest of Honour: Jackson Happy to Take Good with Bad," *Advertiser* (Adelaide), October 3, 2007.

36 Josh Grossberg, "Michael Jackson Announces 'Final Curtain Call,'" *E!* March 3, 2009, http://www.eonline.com/uberblog/b102884_michael_jackson_announces_final_curtain.html (August 14, 2009).

38 Barack Obama, "President Barack Obama Answers a Question about the Death of Michael Jackson in an Interview with the Associated Press," FDCH Political Transcripts, July 2, 2009, http://search.ebscohost.com/login.aspx?direct=true&db=f5h&AN=32V3184170497&site=ehost-live (August 2, 2009).

38 Alan Duke and Saeed Ahmed, "Goodbye Michael Jackson: Star, Brother, Friend, Father," CNN/Entertainment, July 7, 2009, http://www.cnn.com/2009/SHOWBIZ/Music/07/07/michael.jackson.wrap/index.html (September 7, 2009).

39 Bryan Monroe, "Michael Jackson, in His Own Words," *Ebony,* December 2007, 94–109.

SELECTED BIBLIOGRAPHY

Braiker, Brian, et al. "Michael Jackson." *Rolling Stone*, November 27, 2008.

Gates, David, and Raina Kelley. "Finding Neverland." *Newsweek*, July 13, 2009.

Hewitt, Bill, and Alex Tresniowski. "Michael Jackson's Death Drugs, Doctors & Deception." *People*, August 10, 2009.

Jones, Steve. "Michael: King of Pop Dies." *USA Today*, June 26, 2009.

Jones, Quincy. "Remembering Michael." *Newsweek*, July 13, 2009.

Klein, Arnie, and Shaheen Jafargholi. "Encore: Interview with Michael Jackson's Doctor." Interviewed by Larry King, *Larry King Live*, CNN, July 11, 2009.

Lehrer, Jim, et al. "Michael Jackson Dies at Age 50." (Quincy Jones, et al). *NewsHour with Jim Lehrer*, PBS, June 26, 2009.

Montagne, Renee. "Michael Jackson: Child Singer to King of Pop." *Morning Edition*, NPR, June 26, 2009.

People "Growing up Jackson." July 13, 2009.

Robinson, Smokey, Cher, Celine Dion, Sheryl Crow, Kenny Rogers, and others. "Michael Jackson: A Life Remembered." Interviewed by Larry King. *Larry King Live*, CNN, June 29, 2009.

Wickman, DeWayne. "Jackson Lived a Tragic, Yet 'World-Changing' Life." *USA Today*, June 30, 2009.

FURTHER READING

BOOKS

Friedman, Lise. *Break a Leg! The Kids' Guide to Acting &
Stagecraft*. New York: Workman Publishing, 2002.

Grant, Adrian. *Michael Jackson: A Visual Documentary*. London:
Omnibus Press, 2009.

Jackson, Michael. *Moonwalk*. New York: Harmony, 2009.

Reeves, Diane Lindsey. *Career Ideas for Kids Who Like Music and
Dance*. New York: Facts on File, 2001.

WEBSITES

Michael Jackson
    http://www.michaeljackson.com/us/home
    The official Michael Jackson website features his biography,
    photos, and videos.

Michael Jackson: Official Full-Length Music Videos
    http://www.mtvmusic.com/jackson_michael
    This MTV website offers a selection of Michael Jackson videos.

Motown Records
    http://www.motown.com
    Visit the site of the legendary record label that signed the
    Jackson 5 in 1968.

Rolling Stone: Michael Jackson Discography
    http://www.rollingstone.com/artists/michaeljackson/discography
    This page from the popular music magazine *Rolling Stone*
    features a list of recordings released by Michael Jackson.

INDEX

PHOTO ACKNOWLEDGMENTS

The images in this book are used with the permission of: © Jim Steinfeldt/Michael Ochs Archives/Getty Images, p. 2; © Michael Ochs Archives/CORBIS, p. 6; © Tammie Arroy/ AFF/Retna Ltd./CORBIS, p. 8; © Gems/Redferns/Getty Images, p. 9; © Michael Ochs Archives/Getty Images, p. 14; © RB/Redferns/Getty Images, p. 16; © Arthur Schatz/Time & Life Pictures/Getty Images, p. 17; © Bettmann/CORBIS, p. 20; © CBS Photo Archive/ Hulton Archive/Getty Images, p. 21; AP Photo/file, p. 23; © GAB Archive/Redferns/Getty Images, p. 25 (both); © Lynn Goldsmith/CORBIS, p. 26; © Steve Granitz/WireImage/ Getty Images, p. 31; Richard Young/Rex Features USA, p. 34; © Kevin Mazur/AEG via Getty Images, p. 37; Stewart Cook/Rex Features USA, p. 39.

Cover: AP Photo/C.F. THAM.